Contents

KT-146-780

Acknowledgements

This guide could not have been written without the help of many people working in different agencies and projects which are successfully helping disaffected young adults to re-engage with learning. It contains case-study information about twelve particular initiatives which were visited. However it also draws on conversations, reports, documents and photographic evidence from a much larger number of contacts who have been in touch with the Young Adult Learners Project over the last eighteen months. We are grateful to them for taking the time and trouble to inform us about their work and to engage in helpful discussions about it.

The judgements, observations and ideas contained in the guide are in large part our own but they have been shaped by what we have seen and heard from these different sources. It is not possible to recall and record them all so instead we would like to say an open thank you to the staff and young people involved.

We are also grateful to the Local Government Association for funding the Young Adult Learners Project and to the Social Inclusion and Student Support Division of the Department for Education and Employment for supporting the publication of this guide. Like NIACE and the National Youth Agency they are advocates of lifelong learning and intent on ensuring that all members of society are included in pursuing and benefiting from it. We hope that this guide can make something of a contribution to the same policy goal.

Only Connect

Successful practice in educational work with disaffected young adults

Bryan Merton   Allen Parrott

NIACE
THE NATIONAL ORGANISATION
FOR ADULT LEARNING

D/EE
Department for Education and Employment

Published by the National Institute of
Adult Continuing Education (England and Wales)

21 De Montfort Street
Leicester LE1 7GE
Company registration no. 2603322
Charity registration no. 1002775

First published 1999

Produced by the Department for
Education and Employment

The views expressed in ths publication are those of the
authors, and should not be taken to represent the
views of the Department for Education and Employment

NIACE, the national organisation for adult learning,
has a broad remit to promote lifelong learning
opportunities for adults. NIACE works to develop
increased participation in education and training,
particularly for those who do not have easy access
because of barriers of class, gender, age, race,
language and culture, learning difficulties and
disabilities, or insufficient financial resources.

NIACE's website on the Internet is http://www.niace.org.uk

Cataloguing in Publication Data
A CIP record of this title is available from the British Library

Designed and typeset by Boldface

ISBN 1 86201 049 8

Introduction

This guide is designed to benefit those who manage or provide services, projects and programmes for young adults aged 16-25 who have been switched off education, training and work. They can be hard to reach and even harder to teach. At this age all young people are in a phase of transition, seeking the independence and autonomy that comes with being an adult. But for those known as 'disaffected' this journey is more daunting, more protracted and strewn with more difficult obstacles, not the least of which is their own educational under-achievement up to the age of 16. Their lack of key educational and vocational skills may be attributed to their negative experience of school, while their often fractured emotional development nearly always stems from turbulent family circumstances. This combination of educational and social difficulties makes learning of any kind, let alone lifelong learning, an elusive goal.

These young adults pose considerable challenges to practitioners working in the formal and informal education sectors – further education, careers service, vocational training, youth work, adult learning and community projects. Yet across the country professionals in these fields are investing an impressive amount of energy, inventiveness, wit, commitment and resources in developing initiatives which reach out to young people on the margins and seek to bring them back into the social mainstream. This guide is written both as testimony to their efforts and as encouragement to others to do likewise.

It draws on contacts made over the last twelve months with projects, schemes and programmes in all parts of Britain. As the title suggests, we take the view that making connections with the young people as individuals and with the world as they experience it provides the only effective way ahead if we are going to be successful in switching them on to learning.

In Part One we discuss the context of disaffection in the late 1990s. In Part Two we look at what constitutes good and successful practice drawn principally from visits to the twelve projects which provide the case-study material and also from contacts made with a much larger number of agencies. Where the text is in italics it comprises commentary derived from the visits or from this broader range of projects. Finally, in Part Three we widen the focus again to look at curriculum matters, in particular a framework which is being developed by the Young Adult Learners Project to help young adults with low self-esteem acquire the state of learning readiness that will enable them to take advantage of the increasing number of programmes and projects now available to them.

We are grateful to those who sent information and who gave valuable time to host visits. After years in which professional workers have been enjoined to compete, leading not surprisingly to relationships with their peers which have often been predatory and defensive in turn, it is heartening to report a palpable openness and willingness to share experience. The cause of providing a better deal for a group of young people who have been left in the sidings for almost a generation is one which obviously strikes a chord with professionals in all public services. Since this cause has recently become a key aspect of public policy we hope that this guide will prove a timely as well as a useful publication.

'ethos of care and support' ▶
Tower Hamlets Summer University

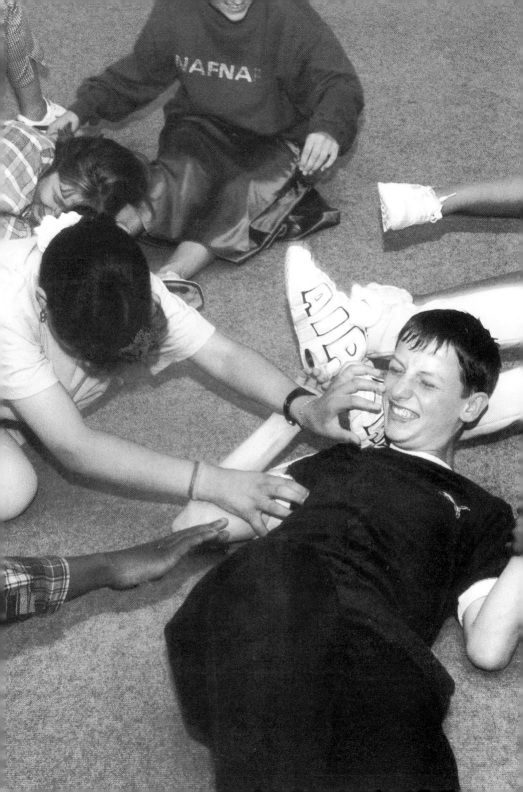

Part One

The context

Policy background

Until recently public policy had failed to recognise that a substantial proportion of young adults was disengaged from education, training and employment. However, soon after its election in May 1997, the Government established the New Deal for 18-25-year-olds who have been unemployed for six months or more, as well as the New Start strategy for 14-17 year olds who have either dropped out of education or are in danger of doing so. In Wales a parallel Youth Access Initiative has been launched. The Kennedy report *Learning Works* (1997) on widening participation in further education also signalled the need for new pathways to learning for groups which do not traditionally take up education and training post-school. The newly-established Social Exclusion Unit and the Parliamentary Select Committee on Education and Employment issued reports during 1998 on truancy and disaffection among 14-19-year-olds, both urging more co-ordinated local action to reduce the numbers of pupils being excluded from school and the setting of targets to monitor and measure how effectively this is done.

The careers service has been steered to work with more focus on the disaffected, while the school curriculum at Key Stage 4 has been loosened up in order to encourage and stimulate a wider range of vocationally-directed opportunities, including enriched programmes of work experience and bridging courses with local further education colleges. The Government has announced the establishment of 25 Education Action Zones expected to pioneer innovative approaches to raising achievement in disadvantaged areas, and LEAs are being required to draw up behaviour support plans. This all amounts to a comprehensive set of initiatives for everyone working in the formal and informal education sectors, whether with school pupils or young adults.

Definitions and causes of disaffection

The particular sources of disaffection for any individual are many and complex, and each young person will have his or her own unique story. When asked, however, most will trace a significant portion of their disenchantment back to unsatisfactory and often unhappy school experiences which frequently culminated in truancy and exclusion. And exclusion from school is closely related to exclusion from many other opportunities later on.

More general causes of disaffection have been widely discussed in recent publications. The Select Committee's report distinguishes between *underlying causes*, such as poverty, inter-generational unemployment, unstable home and family situations, peer group pressure and, most importantly, earlier learning difficulties; and *precipitating* causes, divided into two broad categories. On the one hand, there are in-school factors, such as bullying, teacher attitudes, an inappropriate curriculum and a seemingly irrelevant qualifications system. On the other, there are out-of-school factors like poor job prospects, teenage pregnancy and parenthood, drug abuse and criminal behaviour.

Another report, *Wasted Youth*, published by the Institute for Public Policy Research in 1998 uses the term 'disaffection' interchangeably with 'disengagement'. In seeking to define the phenomenon, the report discusses and rejects the dualism of the sociological concepts of *agency* and *structure* as a way of explaining social patterns. In the first case the young person is seen as the author or agent with prime responsibility for their own life situation, and disaffection would be viewed as a cultural expression of individual attitudes and behaviours; any remedies are likely to be found in sanctions or incentives aimed at changing attitudes and behaviour. In the second case the disaffected young person is seen primarily as a victim of powerful socio-economic forces, and disaffection is viewed as the product of systemic or structural factors which have to be removed or improved if there is to be any change.

For most disengaged young people it is likely that their disaffection arises and continues as a result of some complex interaction between agency and structure. Their main experience of structural factors is likely to be of an education and employment system in which they and their family have not thrived, and, in response, they may well have chosen to adopt attitudes and behaviours which put themselves at even greater distance from it. Even though there may be certain features common to all or most disaffected young people, the specific causes, circumstances and consequences of each young person's disengagement will be different in important ways from any other's. So, without in any way denying the important causative role of structure in the creation of youth disaffection, we must report that all of the successful programmes and projects investigated for this guide focused mainly on individual approaches – on the idea of young adult learner as agent.

In the widespread public debate about what has come to be called 'social exclusion', disaffected young adults have also been referred to as 'the lost generation' or in 'Status Zer0'. Such dramatic labelling is controversial, in part because it suggests the emergence of a distinct youth underclass and also because it implies polarisation and rigidly oppositional attitudes. The actual picture seems to be more complex and more fluid with many young people moving in and out of main-stream society at different times. Moreover, not everyone who is disengaged is also hostile to education and some are described as 'passively disaffected'. Nevertheless most are, and will need no prompting to assert that "learning sucks", as they turn their backs on conventional programmes and provision.

The scale of disaffection

The scale of disaffection is hard to measure precisely. In addition to arguments over definition there is a continuing debate about the reliability of the figures frequently cited. The Select Committee's report contains figures derived from secondary school sources. Every year tens of thousands of 16-year-olds leave school without any qualifications. In 1994/5 15,000 Year 10 pupils and 22,500 Year 11 pupils were estimated to be persistent truants, and in 1995/6 a total of 6,253 permanent exclusions were recorded.[1] These numbers are judged to be rising year by year and have caused such consternation that the Government has required local authorities to issue targets for reducing the numbers over the coming years.

Such figures are significant because, as we have seen, experience at school is an important indicator of later disaffection. Those who fail to achieve at school, who may be excluded or who exclude themselves by truanting, or who may be "in school, but out of learning", are the least likely to find their way into education, or training, or work with training, once they have completed the compulsory phase. They are accordingly more likely to find themselves on the margins of opportunities and of the communities in which they live. The *Wasted Youth* report challenges the popular view that disaffection is a largely male issue. Although it is true that school exclusions and criminal activity apply mainly to young men, regular truancy, low school achievement and dropping out of post-school opportunities apply equally to young women as well. While programmes targeted at ex-offenders can therefore expect to have a predominantly male take-up, the majority of programmes are aimed at disaffected young people in general and consequently attract more equally balanced gender groupings.

Measuring disaffection among those who have left school is not easy. Apparently reliable sources used to compile the figures published by the DfEE, such as the Labour Force Survey, the Further Education Funding Council and the TECs, are still disputed. In 1993 researchers in South Wales concluded[2] that between 16 per cent and 23 per cent of the 16-18 cohort were at any one time in Status Zer0. The Select Committee's report gave estimates[3] of non-participating 16-18-year-olds ranging from 162,000 (9 per cent) of the cohort to 190,000 (16 per cent). Since young people move in and out of disaffection accurate estimates of numbers will always be difficult.

Another approach is to count the numbers of 18-25-year-olds who are unemployed and claiming benefit. The size of this group has shrunk considerably since the New Deal was first announced.[4] Before May 1997 there were reputed to be about 250,000 of this age group who were eligible for the New Deal. By August 1998 it appeared that about half this number had found their way back into work or training. However, there are thought to be thousands who are not registering as unemployed but who may still be marginalised and disaffected.

Whatever their particular circumstances and however large the overall problem may be, most of these disaffected young people remain hard to reach. They nearly always have low levels of self-esteem, motivation and expectation. Some are highly visible – on street corners, in parks and in shopping precincts; others remain invisible, staying indoors, perhaps as lone parents or young carers. Reaching these disaffected young people and providing them with appropriate learning opportunities, in tune with their needs and aspirations, is a challenging task. That it can be done successfully is testified by the examples of good practice that follow.

---

1   DfEE Evidence from DfEE Statistical Press Notice 30.10.97. *Permanent exclusions from school in England 1995-6. Excellence in Schools*, Cm 3681, p. 79.

2   Young People Not in Education, Training or Employment in South Glamorgan, Istance, Rees & Williamson, South Glamorgan TEC and University of Wales, Cardiff (1994).

3   Figures quoted by DfEE in Memorandum to Select Committee's Enquiry on Disaffection.

4   From New Deal for a Lost Generation, Road to the Manifesto, Labour Party (1996).

'democratic, participatory, enjoyable and relevant' ▶
Tower Hamlets Summer University

Part Two

Successful practice

In the following pages successful practices with disaffected young people are described under five broad headings:

1 Reaching Out – approaches to recruitment, targeting and retention
2 Bringing In – programmes of activity that work
3 Putting Across – effective approaches to teaching and learning
4 Achieving Together – assessment and accreditation methods
5 Working With – professional partnerships and inter-agency support

This selection of themes is not arbitrary. It encompasses those aspects of planning, management and provision which present the greatest challenge to providers of education and training.

There is of course one conspicuous omission from the list above: funding. There are two reasons for this. First, the DfEE has already produced a report entitled *Funding Sources for Projects for Disaffected Young People* from its Quality and Performance Improvement Division (1998). This contains a map of the different sources of funding available, specifies the levels of funding and the access criteria, identifies pointers for good practice and gives advice on how to prepare and make bids and to manage the funds. Anyone contemplating a project or programme for disaffected young people would be well-advised to use the report alongside this guide.

There is little we could add by way of information or advice. We would, however, point out that until recently many initiatives have been

Figure 1

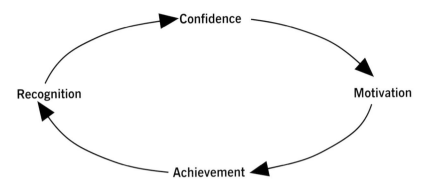

dogged by the problems of short-term, competitive funding or 'the dash for cash', much of which has been excessively outcome-related, and has rarely been conducive to good practice. Second, this guide is intended primarily to indicate how to attract disaffected young people to learning and keep them interested. Its centrepiece is an account of those processes of teaching and learning which have proved most likely to motivate young people and replace a vicious spiral of failure with a virtuous circle of achievement. (See figure 1)

The guide has been researched and written in the belief that practitioners can learn usefully from the experience of others operating with broadly similar target-groups. Given sufficient imagination, flexibility and determination, it may often be possible to transplant principles and practices from one situation where they have worked to another which at first glance looks very different. This guide is a distillation of the stories told by youth workers, careers advisers, college lecturers, school teachers, social workers and probation officers up and down the country. What they had and have in common is a desire to do something about the seemingly intractable problem of motivating and sustaining disaffected young adults on education and training programmes. Our hope is that anybody else wrestling with the same problem and wishing to make a positive contribution in their own locality will find these experiences relevant and useful.

Reaching out – approaches to recruitment, targeting and retention

Outreach

Since disaffected young adults are a most difficult group to attract to formal learning programmes, many projects stress the importance of informal outreach work and informal contacts on the streets as a way of reaching them. For example in Bolton,

> *Initially staff would just make contact with the groups, making themselves known, making small talk and just trying to get the gang members to feel comfortable. It was important at this point for the young people to experience acceptance of them as themselves.... and also important to know when workers' company was not welcome.*
> (Bolton College, YSP – Youth Skills Preparation – Project)

More formal outreach methods have also been successfully used:

> *The Double Take project in Warwickshire, initiated by the local careers service, contacted 600 people over a period of two-and-a-half years using outreach strategies which included:*
> - *visiting young people at home whose post-statutory education destination was unknown to the careers service and who had not responded to telephone calls or mail-shots*
> - *the provision of mobile offices on isolated housing estates and villages.*

Over this period outreach careers advisers built up relationships with young people and gave them the information, advice and support they needed to make decisions about future options.

Outreach work can be time-consuming and frustrating for the worker, because initial contacts are sometimes hard to follow up. Young people may promise to meet on a subsequent occasion at an agreed time and place, but then fail to show up. Workers need to be patient, resilient and able to deploy inter-personal skills of a high order. For many projects, especially in their early stages, there is no substitute for going to where the young adults are, and gaining their trust by talking with them.

In the Bolton project, where there was a strong local gang culture, the worker only succeeded when he won over one of the gang leaders.

Eventually, a YSP outreach worker met Imran on his own and although he said that he would be willing to give the programme a try he was very concerned that the other gang members would ostracise him for his actions. A couple of weeks later another member agreed to enrol on YSP and at this point Imran found it acceptable to join as well. Contact with the gang was maintained. More than half the members eventually joined YSP...

Initial contacts

The passage just quoted illustrates the importance of the initial contact. By definition, any young person who is disaffected is likely to be suspicious of anything that smacks of education or officialdom. These early contacts must therefore be characterised by respect for the person and a willingness to listen to their needs and aspirations. They must be genuinely empathetic encounters without any condescension on the part of the project worker, but also without condoning anti-social behaviour or colluding with the negative attitudes which are frequently expressed. This can be a difficult balance to strike.

Most of the projects investigated have developed a policy in which the initial contact with a potential learner consists of a very informal initial conversation, which is more like a chat than an interview. In the process clear messages about the programme will be given to the young person, and in turn the project worker will be listening very carefully to their hopes, and sometimes their fears. The focus of such friendly dialogues is on future possibilities rather than on past or present experiences and failures. Any assessment or selection going on is likely to be mutual or two-way. While the project worker may well be making all kinds of useful educational judgements about the young person, such initial assessment will be of no practical use if the latter decides during the conversation that the project and its programme is not going to be right for them.

In the St. Helens Youth Service's 'Training for Life' initiative recruitment is by referral, usually of young people who have not completed Youth Training programmes who are referred by the local TEC or careers service. A meeting is set up for the young person, the referral worker, a parent or guardian and a youth worker. The project is explained to everyone and at the end of the meeting a decision is made on whether this opportunity is the right provision for the young person. If so, a contract is signed committing the young person to thirty hours a week for twelve weeks. If not, the young person is referred elsewhere.

Incentives and attractions

Even if all initial suspicions are overcome, the young person is likely to face the project worker with the potentially difficult question, 'what's in this for me?' Many reply by emphasising the importance of acquiring key skills and talk enthusiastically about the opportunities on offer or the chance to try again with a clean slate. This approach may not be sufficiently convincing.

Some successful projects have also addressed this question in a very pragmatic way – by offering not just free course programmes but also additional financial incentives.

On the basic skills scheme in the Open Learning Centre at Pontypridd College cash incentives were found to have 'magical powers' as far as recruitment was concerned. Participants were offered:
- *all their travelling expenses*
- *an additional £10 per week on top of benefits*
- *a cash reward of £50 on completion of their first Wordpower award, and a further £50 on completion of their first Numberpower award.*

In this case payment by results did much to stimulate and sustain motivation.

As well as incentives of this kind, programmes have found that people can frequently be enticed into a centre, and from there onto a programme, by various other attractions. Sometimes these are an integral part of the programme's content or purpose; for example the motor bikes off-road and on-track at the Newham Docklands Motor-cycle Project, or the offer of free driving lessons in various *Skilled!* projects managed by the Community Education Development Centre in Coventry which combine youth work with basic skills tuition.

In Southwark an outreach worker supporting Somali refugees was concerned by the high levels of disaffection and aggression shown by young men in the community. Knowing they were interested in football he encouraged a former member of the national team to run training sessions each week, and a growing body of young men emerged showing an interest not only in their sporting achievements but also in their culture and the new society they were coming to know. Some of these young men have now become volunteers and support a homework club for their younger peers designed to improve their basic skills. Football is not only a counter to disaffection but also, in combination with other activities, is stimulating educational achievement and pride in the community.

In other projects, the initial attractions which bring young people to a centre in the first place are incidental to the programme itself; they are designed quite literally to bring young people in from the streets.

At the Derby Youth House, the offering includes free snacks, hot drinks, video games, pool, snooker, table-tennis, washing and drying machines, creche facility, trips out, information, and support and advocacy services for people in trouble. These very practical facilities are highly valued by the young people because they improve the quality of their lives in simple straightforward ways. Such provision gives a clear message that their everyday needs are recognised and responded to, and this makes the young people more likely to try out the other opportunities provided, such as group-work, education and training programmes.

CASE STUDY 1

DAYTIME POTENTIALS, DERBY YOUTH SERVICE

This project grew out of the need to provide some daytime activity for people staying at a bail hostel and it provides a safety net for disadvantaged young people from across the city. It meets on three days a week from 12 until 2.30.

The project is based at Derby Youth House in the centre of the city and has three regular staff who are supported by specialists, such as a counsellor on sex and health matters.

The core activity is group work to develop personal skills and confidence in areas such as parenting, job search, and mental health. Increasingly the group has been developing more structured programmes leading to work-related qualifications and certification in, for example, health and safety, IT and fork-lift truck driving.

Experience in the project has shown that there are four elements which need to be in place to assist and support people back into education and training:

1   fieldwork contacting individuals on their own patch in order to discover what might help them best
2   non-threatening initial sessions following this contact which meet the needs of individuals, such as portfolio preparation if they want to return to learn
3   availability of guidance and advice on money and benefits
4   a ladder of progression to further learning delivered as flexibly as possible

The project is part of the Gateway phase of the New Deal. One of its strengths is the links forged with other agencies from which young people are referred and to which they are passed on if they have particular needs. Another key feature is the staff, some of whom have themselves been through the same experiences as the users. They serve as effective role models, demonstrating that some of these problems can be overcome and that the young people can emerge from the project as more capable and independent.

Other publicity

In several projects the production of high quality leaflets, the use of local media and other familiar publicity material were instrumental in attracting people to their projects.

> *The East Leeds Family Learning Centre is successful at recruiting young adults who missed out on learning first time round with a combination of:*
> - *high quality promotional materials sent to carefully selected local households;*
> - *good quality leaflets and brochures with a hard vocational message;*
> - *one-off events like open days and job fairs;*
> - *regular recruiting drives.*

However, conventional approaches to promoting adult education, such as open days, prospectuses in libraries, newspaper advertisements and mail-shots, do not generally attract young people directly. So it is important either to deploy other methods, such as outreach work, or to aim these traditional forms of publicity at family members or local professional agencies in the locality who may be in a position to refer disaffected young people onto programmes.

Targeting

The Family Learning Centre in East Leeds has used data collected by different local authority departments to develop sophisticated targeting techniques.

> *All benefits (housing, welfare, disability) can be combined on one form and to this database can be added other factors contributing to disadvantage – such as poor SATS scores. The data can be colour-coded for households and be used to map those most in need. Then accurate targeting takes place…*

In East Leeds the targeted population comprises the broad category of 'disadvantaged' people. In other projects the target groups are more narrowly defined. For example, in East Birmingham the 'Youth into

CASE STUDY 2

EAST LEEDS FAMILY LEARNING CENTRE, LEEDS CITY COUNCIL

The Centre is a unique partnership between the Council, local colleges of further education and the family of schools, and a number of agencies in the Seacroft area of East Leeds. It has been designated as Britain's first Second Chance School and is part of the European network. It opened in 1996 and has been successful in attracting over 2000 local people to education and training.

The Centre provides the usual range of adult learning opportunities, including short courses in leisure time activities. However, its main impetus is helping people into work and work-related training. Considerable resources have been invested in IT because local people recognise that competence and confidence in handling these new technologies are essential elements of employability.

The programmes are not limited to helping people learn how to manage specific software packages but how to develop more universal IT skills such as CAD and Internet.

The Centre is seen by local FE colleges as a providing access to their provision; for example, Thomas Danby College has secured 1500 enrolments through the Centre, and other specialist colleges in art and design and technology also regard its provision as a significant entry-point.

Staff take time and trouble to discover what companies want from their employees and design customer-specific programmes accordingly. The Centre has consequently set up a Key Skills Unit and a Job Placement Programme, the latter being a scheme which puts the learner straight into work and builds skills training around the experience.

Each learner who wishes to obtain or move into employment has a caseworker who assesses needs and interests at the start of the programme and continuously monitors and reviews progress. The costs of this individual attention are underwritten by the LEA.

Employment' project targeted groups with specific characteristics: minority ethnic groups, young people who had left school without qualifications, those leaving care, the homeless, and lone parents.

Other targeted groups from within the broad category of disaffected, excluded and disadvantaged have been identified and prioritised by projects in different parts of the country. These include women with young children, excluded pupils, ex-offenders, drug users, abused family members and people with mental health difficulties.

In Newham, as in the Bolton example above, the original target group was identified by its physical location rather than by any particular known problems. The target was the young people who hung around the local chip shop and were blamed for vandalism and graffiti. Later on, unsurprisingly, it was found that young people in this group were largely disaffected, at risk and excluded.

Word-of-mouth recruitment

Whichever group of young people is initially targeted by a project, once it has been running for a while the best recruiting agents by far are those who have had a good experience on the programme. Some leaders of projects which have been running successfully for several years find that they can now rely entirely on word-of-mouth recommendations and on continuous referrals by a local network of informal and formal agencies. If previous attenders are also satisfied customers they are going to be a project's most persuasive and credible advocates.

Retention

Once a young person has been successfully recruited it is important that their motivation is sustained. The initial incentives or attractions may not be sufficient in themselves. The programme itself must provide day-by-day reinforcement, so that the reasons for the young person continuing to attend are to a significant extent internally rather than externally derived. The programme, if it is going to achieve its aims, must become an important part of the lives of all those who are participating in it.

**'satisfied customers are going to be a project's most persuasive and
credible advocates'**
Pre-employment Training Project, Hertfordshire

Many project staff report how frequently they have to visit young people's homes to get them out of the house and onto the programme. Many disaffected young people have never acquired the discipline of making routine, everyday commitments. Sometimes the young person responds well to such knock-up home visits, and recognises that they are being supported beyond the normal call of professional duty. In other cases the time and effort invested by staff fails to pay dividends.

To help in the process of developing routines and staying on programmes some projects have developed a mentoring system in which older and more strongly motivated young people will support their younger peers who until now have had little first-hand knowledge of the pressures of being a job-seeking and job-keeping adult.

Often people drop out of programmes because of financial or family pressures, not because of the programme itself. Many project staff emphasised the importance of following up people who drop out, but not for bureaucratic or record-keeping reasons. 'I make renewed contact because they matter, not to check up on them.' Some disaffected young people live in unsupportive families where the other family members have a fixed view about their educational weaknesses and perceived limitations, and no belief at all in their potential as learner or worker. Project managers and programme tutors must recognise such barriers to participation and do what they can to dismantle them, perhaps by making home visits and talking with families.

The other side of the retention coin, however, is dependency. Several projects have found that they were almost too successful for some young people, in the sense that it became difficult to wean them away. Good programmes can develop a family atmosphere, and since many disaffected young people have little experience of a supportive family or of being well-parented, the ties they make with any adult who shows them genuine care can become very strong. In such cases experienced professionals will be aware early on that 'making the break' from the programme might be difficult and will be explicitly preparing the ground with the young person concerned.

'good programmes can develop a family atmosphere'
Pre-employment Training Project, Hertfordshire

CASE STUDY 3

CAREER CLUB, TYNESIDE CAREERS

Career Club is targeted at young people who need extra support in order to get into or return to further education, training or work. There are four such clubs in Tyneside funded by Tyneside TEC.

Young people on average stay in the club for eight to nine weeks and the maximum stay is normally thirteen weeks. They are paid a training allowance for a 21 hour week.

A programme called *The Bridge* is aimed at 16-18 year-olds who have been unable to secure a training place and need some extra support to be able to achieve NVQ Level 1.

Each club has two full-time members of staff. The core of the activity is group work, using materials which have been specifically designed for use by the target-group: a pack, called *Stop, Look and Achieve* which covers four modules – confidence building, interview techniques, job search skills and action planning. The programme has been accredited by National Open College Network.

A new pack is being launched designed to improve the motivation of those who have been disaffected for a long time; it assesses their abilities, strengths and weaknesses.

The Club has been running for almost five years. Numbers coming through each year reach about 400. Positive outcomes into further education, training or jobs run at 70 per cent.

This enterprising initiative by the careers service in the Newcastle area has become something of a model of its kind and is being explored and adapted for use in other parts of the country.

Bringing in – programmes of activity that work

'It's not like school because you find out what you want to know.'

The evidence from the projects confirms that being 'not like school' is an essential characteristic of successful programmes with disaffected young people. Their experience of formal education has nearly always been bad. Schools are places that in their view have contributed to their feelings of inadequacy or failure as far as learning is concerned. All projects, and all programmes within projects, must therefore aim to provide different and better experiences of learning. Programmes 'work' for disaffected young people when they feel more positive about themselves and about their future possibilities. Self-confidence and enhanced self-esteem are the essential and explicit goals.

These goals can be achieved with many different types of programme content and this section describes some of the programmes which have worked. To a large extent, however, it seems to be context rather than content, the hidden rather than the overt curriculum, which will make any project and its learning programmes feel different from mainstream schooling. The personal relationships, the small groups, the individual attention and the ethos of care and support – all the factors explored in the next section of this guide – provide the crucial difference. In fact, the programme content frequently consists of practical, vocational and essential life skills, which are little different from those found in parts of the secondary school and further education curriculum.

In any successful provision for disaffected and socially excluded young people the crucial differences from school are, first, the replacement of an academic and high-status curriculum perceived as difficult and irrelevant by a curriculum that emphasises practical knowledge, skills and personal development; and, second, the practical recognition that learners with a whole complex range of difficulties must receive continuous individual attention and support and this must form a non-negotiable starting-point.

Aims and objectives

A typical aim for a project is that of the Tyneside Career Club: 'To give young people opportunities to develop the confidence and skills to proceed to work, training or full-time education'. Another project aims to 'empower young people in their own development and assist them in maximising their potential and focusing their energies positively'.

All the projects have explicit aims similar to these. It is perhaps worth noting that none of the projects had a more radical agenda. The goal, for better or worse, is to help young people cope with and adapt to society, not to give them the ambition or the tools to change it. Empowerment is seen as an individualistic concept, with no suggestion of disaffected young people working together as a group in order to understand and alter the conditions which lead to social exclusion and inequalities.

General objectives of the kind quoted can be achieved in a variety of ways, and programmes around the country have been developed in response both to local conditions and to the main focus of the initiating agency. Thus college-led projects may start with an adult education or a basic skills model in their mind, so that the young person is given a positive experience of education and training; a careers-led project may place greater stress on guidance and job-search activities, so that participants feel better equipped to apply for jobs; while a project initiated by youth workers might look to emphasise personal development and personal relationships in their programmes, so that the young people feel better and more positive about themselves and survive, if not thrive, in their community and the wider society.

But these various approaches and starting points need be seen only as differences of emphasis. They are in no sense mutually exclusive, especially where agencies are working closely together and making use of each other's expertise. What all successful programmes have in common are learners engaged in activity, a focus on doing rather than listening, and a concentration on practical, personal or vocational content which is demonstrably relevant to the current lives and interests of the participants and to their future careers. In other words, successful programmes are also enhancing the employability of those who take part.

In rural Lincolnshire groups of unemployed young people were contacted by an outreach worker from the Spilsby Youth centre who helped each of them develop a simple action plan based on some basic assessment of their employability. This formed the basis of a portfolio of achievement which graduated from self-esteem through opportunity awareness to skill development. This was then used as a record of their success when interviewed by local employers. The strength of the project lay in the dedication and skill of the youth worker who used his network of contacts with the agencies to extend the provision of opportunities open to the young people.

CASE STUDY 4

SPILSBY YOUTH CENTRE, LINCOLNSHIRE YOUTH SERVICE

Spilsby Youth Centre is located in a small town ten miles from Skegness and 37 miles from Lincoln. Its major sources of employment are agriculture and tourism, both seasonal and unskilled. Young people in the area have low expectations.

The youth centre runs clubs at lunch time, including one for the Duke of Edinburgh Award scheme. It was from this club that the idea for some project work with local unemployed young people emerged.

With financial support from the European Social Fund, the project appointed an outreach worker who has used a core group of disaffected young people as a tool to attract others. By providing information, advice and continuing support in combination with skills as a networker and broker with local agencies, the worker has helped over 80 young people into further education, training or employment. A menu of opportunities has been provided, including careers advice, job search, outward bound, the Duke of Edinburgh Award scheme, an allotment project, and contact with a range of local agencies and employers.

The major issues facing young people in this isolated rural area are health, usually related to substance abuse, and the lack of transport since this severely impairs young people's access to study, work and social amenities.

Another example of good practice and inter-agency co-operation is a college-based scheme in Bolton.

CASE STUDY 5

YOUTH SKILLS PREPARATION, BOLTON COLLEGE

This initiative was prompted by the local TEC asking the college to submit a bid for work with disaffected young people in an area of the town which was the subject of Single Regeneration Budget funding. Considerable numbers of Asian young men were on the streets and a cause of concern to local residents and shopkeepers.

The project is co-ordinated by a local youth worker who in combination with a part-time Asian youth worker managed to persuade young people to take part in a short-course programme at the local college. The incentive was the payment of an allowance of £20 per week on top of their benefits. The students also receive free meals in the college canteen in addition to a contribution towards travel costs.

Currently demand is far outstripping the provision of 40 places a year. There is a roll-on, roll-off programme comprising key and life skills, communications, maths and IT. Additionally there are vocational tasters through in-filling existing courses, (IT is the most popular), sports, work experience and individual tutorials. The programme lasts for 10-15 weeks and is certificated, with different elements accredited by different awarding bodies. Students can end up with three or four awards, more than most of them managed to achieve at twenty hours a week in school.

Most of the work is done in small groups in workshop mode. In communications the focus is very much on helping students talk and listen to each other, share ideas and viewpoints and give people the opportunity to express themselves.

Learning outcomes are agreed at the first meeting with the co-ordinator in which each student develops an action plan. These individual sessions continue throughout the programme as a means of reviewing progress and providing continuous support.

'success came mainly from the attraction of motorbikes'
Newham Docklands Motorcycle Project

Where Bolton College and Spilsby Youth Centre both offer provision which is primarily and openly educational, other providers have successfully used a more indirect approach in which any formal learning or training is apparently incidental to the project's main function or attraction. The Newham Docklands Motorcycle project is an excellent example of effective educational work by stealth.

CASE STUDY 6

NEWHAM DOCKLANDS MOTORCYCLE PROJECT

The project was established in 1993 following research conducted by the London Docklands Development Corporation concerning the lack of resources for local young people. The research revealed that, more than anything else, the young people wanted access to motorcycles.

In its own words the project "aims to empower young people in their own development and assist them in maximising their potential and focusing their energies positively". Key areas of development are technical and inter-personal skills which lead to increased self-worth and a greater sense of responsibility.

The target group is local young people with special educational needs, young people not attending school or college and those at risk. In the main those attending are white, working-class boys and young men. Nearly 3,000 young people have participated in training activities since the project began.

The programme consists of training in mechanics, moto-cross (off-road motorcycling) and mountain biking, pre-driver and road safety. There are also opportunities to do work experience and a voluntary work placement. Most of the work is done in small groups. Formal training leads to City & Guilds qualifications, input into the National Record of Achievement and the project's own certificates. The project is run by three full-time staff and a number of sessional staff and volunteers. As a voluntary organisation it seeks financial support from the local authority, charitable trusts and the private sector.

The clients leave when they finish their training programme and when they feel they have outgrown the project. They develop the key skills of problem-solving and teamwork. The content of the programme is often modified to meet individual needs. A more structured approach is sometimes used with Year 11 school groups, but open-ended programmes are preferred.

This project also inspires loyalty in its young participants, some of whom return to the programme as volunteer helpers. Success comes mainly from the attraction of motorbikes, the willingness to be flexible in the programmes offered and the good local reputation which has been built-up over five years.

Adam was one of the Project's first users. He started when he was 12 after continually getting into trouble with the police for illegal riding and other activities. He did not attend school regularly and was considered to be a certainty for more serious trouble in the future.

At the Project he learned to ride safely and helped out on the track, in the workshop and the office. In 1997 he spent part of his summer doing Youth Training with the Project to improve his awareness of a working environment. His self-confidence and inter-personal skills grew and he found a new dedication to work.

He now has a job as a scaffolding assistant. It's not all easy going. 'I get up at 6 in the morning and have to start at 8, no excuses, but it feels good when I get my hands on my money at the end of the week.' Adam is now determined to work hard and keep his job. He stops by at the Project regularly with progress updates and is now a keen member of the management committee. The Project's work with Adam is recognised and valued by his family and by the wider community.

Another college-based approach is to be very open and direct with young people about the importance of basic skills, especially literacy and numeracy. As the example from Pontypridd indicates, a college taking this line may have to find some kind of material incentive to attract the young learners they are targeting and other agencies are needed to help with recruitment.

CASE STUDY 7

BASIC SKILLS UNIT, PONTYPRIDD COLLEGE

This scheme started when the local TEC contracted with the college to provide 40 places for disaffected 16-25 year-olds under the Training for Work programme. For 1998/9 the scheme will be increased to 170 places and will be funded under the Work Based Training for Adults programme. Young people are mainly referred through the Employment Service, Job Centres and Job Clubs, and recruited via community groups and word of mouth.

The main feature of the programme is the development of basic skills pursued through Wordpower and Numberpower assignments. Individual action plans are drawn up, and as well as developing their communication skills, learners can undertake project work, investigations, vocational tasters, visits, job search and IT training. In the case of projects and visits, learners use telecommunications (phone, fax and e-mail) and are encouraged to exercise independence and project management skills in planning their time, sorting out their travel arrangements, costs and project reports.

After agreeing an individual action plan, learners attend for fifteen hours a week direct tuition, plus off-site assignments. They receive all their travel expenses and an additional £10 per week on top of their benefits. When they achieve their first Wordpower award they receive a £50 bonus and a further £50 for their first Numberpower award – payment by results! Rewards are contingent upon students sticking with their programmes and conforming to some 'simple ground rules'. They can stay on the scheme for up to 52 weeks. Retention rates are high at 94 per cent. Apart from accredited basic skills, the main outcomes for learners are an increase in their self-confidence and in their belief that they can learn. A reduction in offending and alcohol and substance abuse has also been noted.

The programme is staffed by college tutors who take on multiple roles as outreach workers, teachers and counsellors. Guidance is provided in the college and in the community. There is close liaison with other specialist agencies on particular issues or problems. The college counsellor visits the programme weekly, or immediately in cases demanding crisis intervention.

Park Lane College in Leeds offers a range of life skills, and practical learning activities potentially related to employability, in what looks at first sight very like a mini adult education prospectus. But the focus is very much on disaffected young people, including excluded school pupils below the age of 16 in some cases. This provides the opportunity for continuity of provision and, in some cases perhaps, for preventing lasting disaffection by 'catching them young'.

CASE STUDY 8

CROSS GATES AND BURTON ROAD LEARNING CENTRES AND ST ANNE'S CENTRE, PARK LANE COLLEGE, LEEDS

Cross Gates in situated on the outer ring road to the east of Leeds and provides a number of programmes targeted at disaffected young adults. Burton Road Centre provides a similar range of programmes in the inner south area of the city.

Options and Choices has been running for three years and was developed after youth workers approached the college and asked them to provide eight-week courses in the twilight period from 4pm to 6pm. The spur to attend has been the subject matter of the courses – cookery, IT, first-aid, painting and decorating, motor-bike maintenance, baby-sitting – essentially practical skills which improve self-confidence and employability. Accreditation is provided through the local Open College Network.

There is also an initiative aimed at young people excluded from school. About 30 Year 11 pupils are referred and attend vocational courses at college on an in-fill basis for different periods ranging from two to eight hours a week. Progress is reviewed after six weeks. They study for units of accreditation and can log what they do in their Record of Achievement.

The third form of provision is the Open Learning Centre which occupies the second floor of a day centre for the homeless in the city centre. The Centre is dedicated to 16-25-year-olds who are in high risk situations, some of whom are involved in substance abuse and have mental health problems. The provision is a combination of basic, life and social skills, most of it dispensed by highly committed, experienced teachers who develop strong, supportive relationships.

Small group work combined with one-to-one tuition and support are the ingredients which work most effectively. The young people are closely involved in reviewing programmes and one of the factors they cite in their improved motivation and achievement is the opportunity to 'enjoy learning something with a tutor you can talk to'.

There is close liaison with other professionals in setting up and developing these programmes, including youth workers, teachers, and staff from bail and homeless hostels.

Residential activities are an additional element in many successful projects because they sometimes produce a step-change in young people's learning and development.

In the East Birmingham 'Youth into Employment' programme, for example, the main attraction for participants is the residential half-way, which includes many confidence-boosting outdoor pursuits and self-help activities.

CASE STUDY 9

YOUTH INTO EMPLOYMENT PROGRAMME, BIRMINGHAM YOUTH AND COMMUNITY SERVICE

This programme has been running since 1994 in the Hodge Hill and Yardley area of the city. It consists of twelve-week pre-vocational courses each lasting approximately twenty hours a week and aimed at groups of ten to twelve people aged 16-18. Half way through each programme is a residential.

The programmes are run in local youth centres and staffed by a youth worker alongside a trainer. They consist of a mixture of work-related activities such as careers guidance, basic skills and job sampling; and social education activities such as sports, arts and local visits.

Each morning of the main programme is spent on work-related activities and personal development training. In the afternoon the young people take part in leisure and recreational activities. As well as developing basic skills of communication, literacy and numeracy, the programme offers opportunities to develop more practical skills which will enhance employability such as driving, building, health and safety, first aid and the 'softer' skills such as teamwork, confidence-building, and so on .

The work has been funded by the European Social Fund and the local TEC. It is supported by two departments within the council (Economic Development, Leisure and Community Services) and by ENTA, a city-based training provider. The programme has been so successful in the one area of Birmingham that it was replicated in other parts of the city. It has been instrumental in making a successful bid for European Youth Start funds and projects were consequently set up in several parts of Birmingham from September 1998.

Initial assessments

A lot of programmes placed great emphasis on initial and diagnostic assessments with each individual. In these the young person is encouraged to talk about their own personal interests, aspirations or agenda and to explore the things which might help or hinder them in their learning. Questions like 'What helps me learn?' and 'What stops me learning?' encourage the self-awareness which is integral to confidence-building. A patient and skilled interviewer will try to lead the young person from such explicit awareness of self to an awareness of the opportunities available on the programme and of how these connect to the learner's own goals.

In Scotland staff at the Borders Production Unit undertake a comprehensive analysis of each person's training needs during a short period of induction and initial assessment. As these will vary greatly, staff are forced to consider early on in the process any specific arrangements which need to be made for individuals or groups. The young people are full partners in the process, encouraged to offer their own assessment of their abilities, interests, preferences and potential. By actively fostering student participation in the processes and decision making, staff encourage students to take responsibility for their own progress.

The aim of such a session is also to arrive at a set of mutually agreed and achievable learning goals, which might be called a simple Action Plan or an Individual Learning Plan. The Action Plan breaks the learning down into manageable chunks which the individual can realistically achieve.

'teaching and learning styles are probably the most significant factors in determining a programme's success'

A point made by several practitioners is that such initial sessions with individual learners should always concentrate on the possibilities of the future, rather than on the failures of the past. Disaffected young people will be used to the kind of interview in which authority figures explore their past record, while simultaneously filling in an official form, and this kind of interview can be a very dispiriting and demotivating experience.

In the East Birmingham 'Youth Into Employment' programme, as well as giving each young person an initial interview, a short video film is taken of them undertaking an activity. This exercise is repeated at the end of the programme and seeing the two videos helps 'young people recognise how they have grown in confidence'.

Initial Assessment/Induction

Course Aims and Objectives Box
I declare I have received initial assessment and guidance before attending this course and this covered the following areas:
– Background to organization
– Course contents, aims, objectives and structure
– Locations and times of training sessions
– Details of childcare facilities and regulations/requirements when using Crèche facilities
– Financial details for support and costs when on the course
– Conditions of attending the course: timesheets and Attendance
– Health and Safety

The assessment and guidance was provided by

_____ on _____

And involved:

– Introduction to training and nursery staff
– Tour of Crèche, facilities and Training Room and details of other training locations
– Issued with detailed course information pack
– Fire and emergency evacuation procedures
– Course timetable and term table issues
– One to one interviews with course Co-ordinator
– Completed individual participation plan
– Completed beneficiary analysis sheet

Signed: Participant _____ Signed: Co-ordinator _____

Date _____ Date _____

ADDITIONAL SUPPORT COSTS, i.e. childcare, special needs, resources, travel grants etc.

Details			Cost £	

Proforma 1 Daytime Potentials initial assessment form

'young people deserve a well-resourced environment with video, multi-media and IT resources'
Tower Hamlets Summer University

In these examples of programmes that have been effective we have tried to indicate the variety of possible approaches and of formal and informal content available to imaginative programme creators. But all successful programmes depend on the quality of their workers, to which we now turn our attention.

◀ It is important to record what takes place during induction and assessment – key aspects at the start of any programme
Example taken from Daytime Potentials in Derby

Putting across – effective approaches to teaching and learning

Teaching and learning styles and methods are probably the most significant factors in determining a programme's success.

Imagine that you are hoping to initiate a project for disaffected young people in your organisation or neighbourhood and your planning has gone well. Funding has been found and partnerships with other agencies have been established. A cohort of young people has been identified and targeted. Publicity and outreach work have been effective, referrals made and sufficient numbers recruited. Your initial contact with each individual has been pleasing, and a programme is in place that should meet their aspirations, based on effective diagnosis, assessment and action-planning. As project leader you are entitled to feel a small glow of satisfaction as well as a slight tingle of anticipation.

But all that is only the start. It can all go wrong if you do not find the right staff with the right stuff: key personal attributes and professional approaches to their teaching and to the young people's learning.

Successful programmes must feel to the learners as unlike their memories of school as possible. If the young people begin to experience feelings of boredom and failure, or of being patronised and labelled, the programme will be fatally associated with formal education. And it may take only one poor teacher, one moment of sarcasm or one inappropriate comment to cause a spate of early drop-outs.

Teacher attributes

The key ingredient of a successful project, therefore, seems to be the intrinsic personal qualities of the workers and teachers, more than any other single factor. All the projects were pleased with their high retention rates which learners attributed to the excellence of the staff. In the reports the personal qualities mentioned several times include: care, enthusiasm, genuineness, trustworthiness, perseverance, commitment, respect for young people, belief in the potential of all young people to succeed...and a sense of humour. Also, the most effective teachers in these schemes seem to be those who possess the attributes associated with counselling and with youth work, such as the ability to listen and to offer responses which are both non-judgemental and constructive.

Few, however, possess all these qualities all of the time. Perhaps the most that can safely be said is that teachers should not be used on a programme if they appear to be lacking in several of them. However impressive, academic qualifications are largely irrelevant in this context. The important credentials are: first, the ability to make good relationships with 'difficult' young people; and, second, an awareness that there is much more to successful education than the transmission of knowledge and the development of cognitive skills.

Teaching methods and approaches

A large number of the teaching methods used on successful programmes appear in several projects. There is a consensus among those working in this field that the only approach which works well is one based on learner-centred ideas and non-authoritarian practices. There is no evidence that strict regimes involving excessive use of power and authority are successful with disaffected young people. On the contrary, all the programmes investigated for this guide regarded it as axiomatic that learner activities must centre around the individual's perceived needs; and this, as one report put it, *'is a new experience for young people, as it is very difficult for a school teacher to provide this when teaching such large numbers of people'.*

Disaffected young learners appear, therefore, to respond only to that particular style of teaching and learning which will be familiar to experienced adult educators as well as to youth workers: an approach which can be broadly characterised as democratic, participatory, enjoyable and relevant. It may be fitting to express 'good practice' in the form of ten tried and tested prescriptions, or principles:

1   Negotiate as much of the programme as possible, and be prepared to alter plans or strategies which receive the 'thumbs down', even if they have worked well with a previous group or individual. 'Tasters' can test if a topic or activity will be appreciated by learners.

2   Try to find the 'hook' for each individual, the burning issue or interest which will sustain their motivation and which can direct you to relevant course materials for that person – e.g. the kestrel in the book and film *Kes*, or the use of football or pop group texts to support communication skills, or the use of driving to calculate distances, speed, fuel consumption and costs in order to develop numeracy skills. Effective tutors will often produce their own stimulating materials based on local knowledge and on their personal knowledge of individual learners, rather than rely on standard text books or commercially produced worksheets.

3   Avoid lectures or formal inputs, or make minimum use of them, and make sure that any 'guest speakers' are not going to bore their audience. Talk to and with young people, not at them. While it is undoubtedly true that not all learning can be enjoyable or 'fun', that particular lesson is one which these young people have already learned all too well. A successful programme will introduce them to another truth, that some of the most meaningful learning can indeed be both enjoyable and fun. This entails much more activity and much less listening to the teacher than they will have been accustomed to at school – when and if they attended.

4   Keep the groups small. Many programmes report that six to eight learners is an ideal group size, and 12-14 seems to be an absolute maximum for young people who want and need, but are not in the habit of receiving, a great deal of individual attention.

5   Vary the activities and the pace as much as possible, both in the programme as a whole and in the way each class or session is

conducted. Role plays, simulations, working in pairs or threes, individual project work, quizzes and similar 'fun' activities can help to lighten the classroom-based and more serious aspects of the programme. But of course these exercises must also be professional and purposeful. As one report suggested: *'Socially excluded young people (especially those who have basic skills needs) develop sophisticated strategies of perception'.* In other words, they will know if they are being patronised.

6   Young people today, as sophisticated consumers and frequent users of modern technology, are likely to expect – and certainly deserve – to learn in a high quality and well-resourced environment. Thus projects should seek to provide a comfortable base for the taught programme, and also ensure that video, multi-media and especially IT resources will be used during it. Some successful programmes have IT as their core activity. IT is important because young people have to be familiar and competent with new technologies and because the computer can be a "friendly" medium of instruction. It gives information and feedback rapidly and does not make judgements or provoke shame if mistakes are made. Moreover the work produced looks good, so that the finished product can be a source of pride – unlike most hand-written pieces of work.

7   *'A balance needs to be struck between individual and group learning'.* Many project reports made the same point. Although there is no magic formula determining what the proportions should be, the principle of working in both modes is unanimously endorsed. At the start of a programme learners who are shy or withdrawn may only respond to one-to-one support. But participating in a group, provided they are not going to be teased or put down, is an important way of increasing their confidence and self-esteem – the overall goal of all projects. Listening and talking to others, sharing views, leading groups and helping others with tasks are all exercises which are likely to be structured into successful programmes.

8 Some programmes emphasise individual learning styles, and in particular help young people to become aware of themselves as learners. It is important that any individual learning plan or action plan is truly 'owned' by the person concerned; and this process of becoming intrinsically motivated to learn is greatly helped by reflecting on oneself as a learner. *The process of learning must be given as much emphasis as the product.* 'School learning, with its large groups and its emphasis on academic success and failure, can be seen as a particular approach to the learning process which demands a particular learning style. Lack of success at school does not make one a failed learner for all time. *'It is vital that the tutor communicates their faith in the young person's ability.'*

9 Caring for and about these young people may also involve from time to time confronting and challenging them, their attitudes or their behaviour. *'Challenge the behaviour, but don't humiliate the individual'* is a good maxim. The relationships made must be strong enough to cope with honest expressions of feeling as a two-way process; building up in disaffected young people what is now called 'emotional intelligence' is an integral part of the confidence-building process. While tutors or project leaders are likely to provide the main models of the kind of adult behaviour which is being sought, some projects also use older group members to act as mentors or role models for younger newcomers.

10 Working in these ways is extremely demanding, and all teachers on programmes with disaffected young people will need to find their own support. Many programmes emphasise the significance of teamwork and of the mutual support provided by colleagues. If they are to be effective as adult role models, teachers on these programmes must try to ensure that their confidence and self-esteem levels are also high, that they too are self-aware and emotionally competent learners with a positive outlook on the future!

Even if all these prescriptions are heeded and the programme is operating in the ways suggested, there may still be frustrations and disappointments. Young people behave in unacceptable ways from time to time. An unexpected crisis may occur that has nothing to do with the programme itself, but affects the mood and behaviour of an individual or whole group. Some may leave the programme just as a tutor feels that they are beginning to benefit from it, and the reasons for their dropping out may be related to family or financial circumstances, and quite unconnected with the quality of their learning or the merits of the teaching they have been receiving. Yet if a sound working relationship has been made, it can be hard not to take such disappointments personally.

It is important that in such situations staff have support in order to provide an outlet for their own feelings and also to regain a wider perspective. Opportunities should be provided for practitioners to meet and train together, exchange ideas and experiences and harvest the learning from their work.

Disaffected young adults, like all adult learners, will only make significant changes to their lives when they are ready to do so, and when their life situation permits; all that professional workers can ever do is try to ensure that the right kind of learning opportunities are available at the appropriate time. 'It is important to want to do this kind of work but not be a missionary,' said one experienced professional.

Achieving together – assessment and accreditation

While there is general agreement about the most effective approaches to teaching and learning, as discussed in the previous section, there is greater variation of opinion about the best forms of assessment or the most effective ways of recognising young people's achievements on programmes.

All the practitioners consulted agree on the principle of recognition and accreditation of achievement. In practice, however, the different approaches ranged from a policy (found in most college-led projects) of having everything accredited by nationally recognised certification, to the view (expressed by some youth workers) that there are no external qualifications flexible enough for these learners and that projects must therefore create their own internal or 'in-house'

'certificates and qualifications can certainly be an important motivator'
Acorn Initiative Nottinghamshire

certification. These differences illustrate the different institutional contexts and funding arrangements which shape projects and programmes. They also point up an ambiguity in the role of formal assessment where disaffected young people are concerned. Is assessment a motivator or a barrier?

On the one hand certificates and qualifications can certainly be an important motivator, especially after a level of trust has been established and some learning achieved. On the other hand, assessment in general, and exams in particular, may well be a significant barrier in the minds of the young learners themselves, especially at the start of a programme. In schools, as disaffected young people know all too well, assessment is frequently used for other purposes than recognising achievement. It is used to select winners and losers and classify people. Successful programmes, therefore, will be sensitive to this ambiguity and seek to ensure that assessment issues are introduced at the right time and in the right way.

Sometimes this may mean avoiding the issue altogether in the early stages of a programme or of a particular individual's participation, while the right level of trust is being established. In a world where much educational funding did not depend on formally recognised learning outcomes, many programmes were inclined to carry on ignoring the problem of formal assessment, and to focus all their attention on what many regard as the unmeasurable but crucially important business of confidence-building and personal development.

Certainly, the enhancement of self-esteem does not appear an easily measurable concept. However the assessment of so-called 'soft outcomes' is now recognised as an important element of vocational and general education, and there have been some interesting developments in recent attempts to specify learning outcomes and performance criteria in the area of personal development.

All the programmes have sought ways to provide credible and non-threatening forms of assessment that can perform the twin functions of motivating learners and of recognising their learning achievements, thereby contributing to the enhancement of their self-esteem. Many programmes also require a formally recognised accreditation structure in order to secure their own continuing funding, locally or nationally.

Tracking, monitoring and record-keeping

All programmes have some formal mechanisms for reviewing the progress of learners. However, many also place at least equal significance on informal ways of monitoring the learning of young people, based on regular conversations and observations. Even though some programme reports also mention the helpfulness of peer group assessments for particular purposes, the overwhelming emphasis in all programmes is on personalised one-to-one assessments conducted at regular intervals.

Typically reviews of a formal kind take place every four to six weeks. A case-worker or the programme leader discusses the agreed individual learning plan with the young person and together they modify it as necessary. College-based programmes encourage learners to build up a personal portfolio, or record of work done, and these usually provide the basis of mid-course reviews as well as an overall Record of Achievement at the end of the programme. Some programmes such as Intro, offered to young people by the YMCA in Cardiff, also introduce careers advice or suggest new vocational tasters as part of the mid-course review. Learners who have dropped out of the scheme are always followed up on at least one occasion but, as we have seen, this is not primarily for record-keeping purposes but *because they matter.*

In the Training for Life project at St Helens, a review and assessment meeting takes place after each four-week module on the Life and Social Skills programme to ascertain the level of Open College Network (OCN) credits achieved. All the youth workers on the programme have been trained and qualified as assessors through the D32 and D33 awards. As well as OCN certification, the National Youth Agency's record of achievement is also awarded to those who successfully complete the programme.

CASE STUDY 10

TRAINING FOR LIFE INITIATIVE, ST HELENS YOUTH SERVICE

This project was set up in 1995 initially with support from the European Social Fund. It now attracts funding through the Single Regeneration Budget and is therefore confined to one area of the town. TEC funding also supports that element of the programme which gives young people the life and social skills support they need prior to vocational training.

The initiative has two distinct target-groups, those in their last two years of compulsory schooling and 16-18-year-olds who are not yet ready for further education, training or work.

16-18-year-olds undertake a Life and Social Skills programme which lasts for twelve weeks at thirty hours a week. It offers them twelve Open College Network credits at levels 1, 2 and 3. Learning outcomes are clearly specified and the young people can achieve the units at different levels within each of the modules.

The programme is highly participative and the young people are encouraged to establish learning contracts as a group from the outset. Individual action planning for careers forms part of the curriculum. The inclusion of a residential is seen as essential for personal and social development and young people review how well they have participated and achieved through the experience.

The young people are given help with transport and lunches are paid for to ensure basic needs are met. If a young person fails to turn up to a session a youth worker will make a home visit. Follow up and individual support are highly valued by those who take part.

The project is staffed by youth workers who link with specialists from other services such as health and careers. Two full-time youth workers run each programme with support from a half-time worker who acts as tutor, support worker and driver. Access to specialist counselling support is also available. There are close links with schools, social services, pupil referral support, the TEC, the local further education college, careers and health services.

Certificate of Achievement

This is to certify that:

Address of Student:

Has completed a short course in Basic Skills using the Internet.

Skills learned:

- **Launch the Internet Explorer**
- **Go to a specific address on the Internet**
- **Select a Hyperlink**
- **Perform a search on the Internet**
- **Change Search page**
- **Return to Home page**
- **Change Start page**
- **Create Favourite page(s)**
- **Search for text on a page**
- **Copy information from a page to a document**
- **Save information from the Internet**

Signed............................... (Student)   Signed .... (Tutor)

Date ....   Date ....

Proforma 2 from Pontypridd College Certificate Basic Skills Project
**"Certificates of achievement are a tangible record of success –
for some learners it will be their first."**

Skill Areas

Choosing your skill area

You may find it difficult to decide which skill area to choose. Don't worry! It is easier to do than it looks. It should help if you think about what you want your Profile of Achievement to show about you when you have finished the programme.

If you want to use it to help you get a job, then think about the kind of skills you may need to do that job. The same for a college course, training or the job you may be already doing. The choice is yours. Most people find it a good idea to choose a mixture of things they know they are good at with some others that they want to improve a lot.

If, after a couple of weeks, you decide that you would like to change or add to the skill areas you first chose, that's OK. You should give your choices a good try before deciding to make any changes, so think about it carefully and discuss it with your supervisor. They need to know what your targets for achievement are and these are written on your Action Plan.

The skill areas are:
1   Demonstrating a positive attitude
2   Health & Safety Awareness
3   Working as part of a team
4   a) Demonstrating your own personal skills
     b) Development of new skills
5   Using equipment/technology
6   Motivation
7   Using initiative
8   Taking responsibility
9   Problem solving
10 Using and communicating information
11 Caring for others
12 Awareness of the needs of others
13 Perseverance

Proforma 3 Devon Probation Service Skill Areas Form
"Learners should be encouraged to choose the skill areas in which they want to demonstrate their achievement."

Accreditation used in effective programmes

'Home-grown' accreditation can take various forms. In addition to the records of work completed or the portfolios of achievement mentioned above, programmes like the 'Youth into Employment' project in East Birmingham have also offered 'certificates of attendance' and 'certificates of punctuality'; these are often the first certificates these young people have ever achieved. For such learner-friendly programmes it is important that all certificates are not merely awarded but celebrated in some style with food and drink and ceremony. Friends and parents are invited in to celebrate the achievements.

The basic skills project at Pontypridd College also offers its own in-house certificate of achievement which is highly valued by those who receive it.

A systematic approach to accreditation is taken by the Devon Probation Service in a scheme undertaken in partnership with South Devon College which makes the City and Guilds Profile of Achievement central to its whole foundation training programme for ex-offenders – a successful programme which can be described as assessment-led.

> *County-wide foundation training for those on community service orders is accredited using the City and Guilds Profile of Achievement. The young people take 70 hours to complete the award. The training begins with an induction interview in which the students choose five out of thirteen units, two of which are compulsory, and draw up an action plan.... Over a three-month period they compile a portfolio of their achievements and these are reviewed three times.... Half the students are not functionally literate and 90 per cent have never worked. They find the award challenging but achievable and are not deterred by the assessment regime.*

However, more than one programme reports that it assesses in its own way, using internally produced forms of accreditation, because they have found it very difficult to find the right kind of accreditation for their kind of courses..

Scepticism about nationally recognised forms of assessment is more explicit in programmes led by youth workers than in programmes initiated by formal education providers. Professionals in the latter may feel that they have no choice in the matter, given that their funding arrangements usually demand that students acquire vocational or recognised skills qualifications. With a sensitive approach and a careful selection of appropriate qualifications to offer virtue can be made of this necessity, as many successful college-based projects and community education initiatives can testify.

In Oldham the local community education service has set up a 60-hour music technology programme based in the town centre. It recruits young people aged 16-30 who are either referred or refer themselves from the needle exchange, mental health projects, disability schemes, probation and after-care, homeless projects and the careers service. The programme covers basic drum machine patterns and programming, use of four-and eight-track recording equipment, live PA work and guitar, drums and keyboards – and a unit of Wordpower. The students complete a portfolio recording their achievements, overseen by an adult education worker. The course is constantly being modified in the light of student evaluations.

In addition to the well-known basic skills qualification, Wordpower, the Oldham Sound Shop project has made use of the local OCN to provide accreditation for its learners. The flexibility which characterises OCN qualifications has proved beneficial in many projects in all parts of the country.

The advantage of OCN accreditation is that it is customised to the requirements of the local project and to the needs of the learners; units are designed by the project workers to take account of what can realistically be achieved in the time available. Also, there are clear lines of progression for the learner to follow on completion. And since local Open College Networks are part of a national network, the awards achieved by the learners can have wider currency and be recognised as having equivalence with better-known national qualifications like GCSE, GNVQ and NVQ. Furthermore, although there is extra work involved in producing such locally-written programmes and in submitting them for validation, because each new OCN programme always has to be recognised and validated by a panel of peers as a quality assurance measure, the whole process can also be seen as a very useful way of tapping into a local network of experience and expertise; not just of the OCN workers themselves, who are usually helpful in the writing stage, but also of the many other local professionals who will certainly have an interest in providing quality learning for this target group if they are invited onto an OCN validation panel.

Among the formal certification and vocational qualifications most commonly offered to disaffected young people in successful programmes are:

- City & Guilds Wordpower and Numberpower
- CLAIT (IT qualification)
- Key Skills (City and Guilds, Edexcel, RSA)
- City and Guilds Profile of Achievement
- First Aid
- Health and Safety
- Open College Network (OCN) certificates
- Driving Test /HGV/ Motor bike/ Fork-lift trucks qualifications
- Sports Awards (bronze, silver and gold)

Working with – professional partnerships and inter-agency support

Educational under-achievement goes hand in hand with a whole cocktail of social difficulties in the lives of most disengaged young people. It is now commonly recognised by policy-makers, programme and service managers and practitioners that no single agency can tackle successfully the various problems associated with youth disaffection. Joined-up problems require joined-up solutions. The projects which have produced such a rich vein of material for this guide are the outcomes of partnerships, both strategic and operational, in which agencies have acknowledged that they can provide a more effective service and better value in combination than they can on their own.

> 'It is important to make contact with as many community organisations and voluntary groups as possible, even those which may seem only vaguely relevant... Good working relationships need to be formed and maintained particularly with pro-active organisations... It is important to form good relationships with the other agencies even if organisations are trying to achieve similar aims and some appear "self-protective". Competition in an area confuses those who live there and is counter-productive.'
> (Careers Adviser, Dorset)

The aim of networking is not just to help with recruitment, or with the 'selling' of the programme. With disaffected young people as the target group any such marketing metaphor is totally inappropriate. The programmes discussed in this guide are not like products aimed at consumers in a market place, because they stem from deeper human needs and different values. The hope is that the lives of a particular group of young people can be irrevocably changed for the better by the kind of fully human engagement that characterises the best educational experiences. So the aim of networking is to obtain all possible ways of supporting these young people before, during and after their time on the programme, and to ensure that the process of personal change and development is given every chance to become deeply rooted in their world outside any classroom or workshop.

Many young disaffected and socially excluded young people, in whatever group is targeted, will be well known by a number of the statutory and voluntary organisations operating in their neighbourhood. Potential providers of support, guidance and useful ideas or information include the Employment Service, social services, housing, probation, police, careers, drugs action teams, NACRO and Foyer projects, church organisations, youth services and many other community projects or voluntary groups.

In setting up partnership arrangements, it is important that all the agencies involved have a shared vision and a shared understanding of what each partner has to offer and of the constraints which each is working under.

'When starting this work (with disaffected young people) I was determined that any work would be as a direct response to local needs. So I set up a series of meetings with the Youth Service and a local charity called Homeless Young People in East Dorset (HYPED). These meetings suggested the need for both of these organisations to be updated of changes in the way that the careers service has been forced to work ... before any shared ways forward could be identified.'
(Careers Adviser, Dorset)

As a result of such meetings the careers adviser was able to gain access to a sub-culture of disaffected young people who were well known to the youth and charity workers but who had not been turning up to careers appointments arranged for them, and from that opening she could start to develop a programme that would meet their needs. At the same time some mutual training of professional and voluntary workers was taking place during the series of inter-agency meetings. Partnerships of potential benefit to all parties, and therefore to local clients, were being forged.

In Bolton the co-ordinator of YSP brought together the various agencies involved in streetwork in the area of benefit to ensure that information about young people was passed on and duplication of effort and resource was minimised. This also enabled the specialist knowledge and skills of the different agencies (social services, housing authorities, police, drug action teams, youth workers) to be pooled in support of the young people. The involvement of neighbourhood groups was instrumental in getting the communities on-side.

One of the most common partnerships, which has led to many successful programmes, is between youth workers and further education lecturers, especially basic skills tutors.

The different programmes run for different groups of disaffected young people by Park Lane College in Leeds would not have worked without the close cooperation of local youth workers.

The success of the ten Skilled! projects run by the Community Education Development Centre (CEDC) was due in the main to the partnerships created between youth workers and basic skills tutors. Young people's literacy and numeracy skills were developed through activities like music or motor vehicles which they found inherently enjoyable and stimulating.

In those programmes where more than two agencies are active partners, in the operational sense of working face-to-face with the young people, careful co-ordination is obviously required.

CASE STUDY 11

TRANSITIONS INTO WORK, OLDHAM YOUTH AND COMMUNITY EDUCATION SERVICE

This programme was initiated by the local authority social services department and is aimed at young people aged 16 to 19 who are leaving care and in transition to independent living. It is funded by the European Social Fund and is characterised by strong inter-agency links with regard to the planning of programmes and the support and development of the young people.

The project is situated in a small house in the town centre which serves as a youth and community education centre. It is open on five mornings a week from 9.15 to 12.45. It provides structured programmes of personal development and orientation to the world of work and the wider community which last for thirteen weeks.

The programme is designed to build self-confidence through profiling, the provision of information and advice, the development of planning and decision-making skills, individually selected courses of study and group activities. One of the key elements is work experience for which young people are carefully prepared and well supported. The local careers service is closely involved in arranging this. A second key element is a community-based project which serves to widen networks for young people and build their self-esteem and interpersonal skills.

Each young person has a mentor who helps with careers profiling and action-planning. The mentors are in everyday contact with careers advisers and the social services after-care team to ensure that information is shared and the young person gets all the support required.

There is a single project co-ordinator, a team of part-time staff who act as mentors and support from careers advisers and social workers.

When considering partnerships, the public sector agency which is likely to be initiating any local project may find it useful to think beyond the confines of colleagues in other public services. Greater financial support and political influence may be found in private sector partnerships.

Transitions into Work   **Individual Review**
(Please complete weekly)
Date: _____

Name of Participant: _____

Name of Mentor: _____

Topic for review

I can

What I want to try next

How I will do it	How it went

Other things I learned

– about myself

– about others

Signed _____(Participant) _____(Mentor)

This form is the property of the participant and mentor

Proforma 4 Individual review sheet from Oldham, Transitions Into Work
"A critical success factor is the frequent and open communication between young person, mentor and key worker about progress and problems."

CASE STUDY 12

CARDIFF YMCA TRAINING AND YOUTH WORK PROGRAMMES

This programme caters for a mixture of young people, mainly in the 18-24 age-range, including graduates, the homeless, and those who do not 'fit in' and are referred from a number of different sources. A large percentage are young care leavers and drug users, including alcohol abuse. The main way to reach these young people is through outreach as they do not trust institutions and do not respond to leaflets and posters.

There are three main forms of provision.

1. Informal youth work comprising discussion groups and workshops on health and social issues; support and advocacy for individuals; work on the streets and in the hostels.

2 *Intro* lasts from three to fifteen hours a week on a flexible basis and offers assessment, action-planning, basic skills, the RSA CLAIT Level 1 and help with CVs and job search

3 Formal accredited courses of three and four weeks on computers (CLAIT), literacy (City & Guilds), counselling skills (OCN), community first aid (St Johns Ambulance) and job reach through portfolio building (OCN).

The spur to motivation seems to lie in the one-to-one approach and the emphasis placed on building self-esteem. The staff tackle young people's needs and interests holistically, seeing them as individuals in the round and offering them variety and flexibility. The balance of individual and small group work is attractive and effective. Young people are helped to achieve by being encouraged to work and progress at their own pace.

The progress of young people is monitored monthly with each young person closely involved in the process. Accreditation is seen as helpful; not only does it release funding and secure partnerships, but for the individual young person it clarifies goals and builds self-esteem.

In order to make this programme effective, links with a wide range of agencies have been formed. These include: the local authorities, the TEC, careers companies, colleges, drug agencies, hostels, employers, prison and probation services, social workers, Employment Service and voluntary organisations. This exemplifies the commitment to an approach which seeks to apply integrated solutions to inter-related problems.

In all these partnerships it has been crucial to identify precisely what each partner brings to the table: what resources (people, plant, money); what information, knowledge or skills; what networks or contacts that can be shared in order to enrich the offering to the young people. And in combination the partners are then in a position to exert leverage on other sectors and sources of support, including finance, such as the Single Regeneration Budget or EU funding streams.

Once partners have established such essential principles as commonly agreed aims, underpinned by shared values, and a willingness to work together even at the expense of subordinating normal priorities for the greater good of the project as a whole, there remain factors of detail which may determine the success or otherwise of the partnership.

- Each partner should play to its particular strengths.
- Clear boundaries will bring focus to the work and avoid duplication of effort and resources.
- Co-ordination in planning programmes and ensuring adequate resources for them must be supplemented by clarity about reporting structures and processes.
- Agreement about the intended beneficiaries, where they are located, how they should be reached and what clear targets are going to be established for them. Baseline data about their abilities and attainment levels needs to be shared therefore. Agreement about how to measure whether targets are being achieved and on all quality assurance procedures, including who will undertake them and who will receive reports.
- Agreement on monitoring, record-keeping and follow-up procedures for the project: how the learning of the young people and progress on their action plans will be recorded and tracked during and after the programme.
- Clear and open lines of communication, as well as a willingness to share all information about the young people.
- Agreement about staffing costs and arrangements; their deployment, support, training and development in order to meet the aims of the project.

From this it is clear that partnerships are more than a collection of agencies prepared to put their names to a funding bid. They are working organisations with clear tasks and responsibilities which need fostering at different levels, if strategic and operational decisions are to be taken, put into action and fully reviewed in the light of experience. All the partners must be whole-hearted in their commitment. Partnerships need time, care, nourishment and more than a little accommodation of interests and perspectives if they are to work harmoniously. A bad partnership will have an adverse effect on the experiences of the young people. Conversely, good partnerships do much to ensure that the needs of young people can be met holistically; and where the holistic approach is effectively implemented their prospects of success in learning and in work are that much more greatly enhanced.

'effective teachers possess the ability to listen and to offer responses which are non-judgemental and constructive'
Pre-Employment Training Project, Hertfordshire

Part Three

Getting connected

A curriculum for personal development and social inclusion

'In a world where governments no longer exercise much sovereignty either over their defences or over their economies, the best service they can perform for their citizens is to help them be stronger, more responsible, more capable of making decisions and understanding the worlds in which they live. Narrowly this means providing them with skills to make them employable; the habits of being disciplined and flexible, creative and adaptive… More broadly it means helping them to look after themselves and to care for others, helping with life skills and emotional intelligence rather than just the analytical intelligence that older educational systems valued so highly.'
Geoff Mulgan *Life After Politics* 1997

In this final section we focus once more on the wider picture, on the kind of curriculum which is best suited to re-connect disengaged young adults to the mainstream, and on the implications of such a curriculum for mainstream schools and colleges. As Mulgan suggests in the passage quoted above, 'getting connected' is not simply about catering for people who are currently on the margins of our society; it needs to be seen as a fundamental purpose of the entire, lifelong education system, the essential basis of future social cohesion and of individual citizenship in the post-industrial world now being created. If notions like lifelong education or 'the learning age' are to develop into meaningful practices, there will be a new curriculum agenda for policy-makers to consider. From the preceding sections it is possible to infer much of this agenda; we end this guide by making it more explicit.

In a recent research publication, *The Attributes of Youth*, produced by Andersen Consulting in collaboration with the Prince's Trust Volunteers, a significant gap is revealed between the qualities employers are looking for when recruiting young people and those which young people think employers want. Employers want attributes like enthusiasm, initiative, a willingness to learn and inter-personal skills, but the young people think that formal qualifications are the principal requirement. This affects how young people present themselves at interview, and when they 'paint a picture' of themselves they rarely display the attributes being sought. The introduction of key (formerly core) skills into some parts of the formal school curriculum over recent years is a welcome development, but it has not yet diminished the popular view that paper qualifications are all that really count. It is also questionable whether key skills, as currently understood and implemented, go far enough in promoting the attitudes and the ways of thinking and of acting that are required in the modern world of work.

A curriculum is needed which will promote personal development by focusing on the formation and development of attitudes and attributes as much as on skills and knowledge. It is the logical response to the demand from employers for more rounded, enterprising and independent young workers. More importantly it is what young people themselves need and deserve from a compulsory education system which is imposed upon them. Building confidence and self-esteem should be regarded as part of an educational entitlement, so that each young person can present themselves to the world either as 'learning-ready', if pursuing education and training, or as 'job-ready', if employment is the preferred option.

We have seen that for a significant minority of young people extra help is required to get them to this starting gate of learning-readiness and job-readiness. Motivating disillusioned and under-achieving young adults to take the first steps in their own lifelong learning process is a major challenge, for all the social and personal reasons already discussed. Yet, paradoxically, some disaffected young adults, in learning to survive on the margins, also begin to exhibit the kind of guile, resourcefulness and native intelligence which belies their educational under-achievement. From a most unpromising starting point, comprising social problems and emotional turbulence, a few manage to become, with or without help from the kind of programmes discussed in this guide, the kind of self-starters, problem-solvers and independent learners which employers say they are looking for. It is high time that connections were made between the lessons provided by this kind of 'real life' and the formal education curriculum.

The Young Adult Learners Project is designing a curriculum framework which addresses many of the issues outlined above: a curriculum which is more sensitive to the social characteristics which shape young people's lives; a curriculum which takes seriously the qualities asked for by employers; and a curriculum which provides a coherent alternative to the current model of 'hard' academic and vocational outcomes prescribed by the national qualifications framework and required by funding bodies.

A distinctive curriculum for young adult learners

The curriculum developed by the Young Adult Learners Project has one major premise: that young adults are unique individuals with different needs, interests, abilities and aspirations, and that their individuality and uniqueness must inform any learning that is going to be meaningful to them. But at the same time it also asserts that young people cannot develop an individualised curriculum on their own. So the notion of mentoring is absolutely central to the project. It is envisaged that each young learner will have a trusted mentor with whom they will decide the particular combination of outcomes they wish to achieve and the particular learning activities that will help them reach their goals.

The curriculum framework requires the mentor to be both guide and assessor: to be inventive in setting up activities which will allow learning achievements to be demonstrated, to be observant in

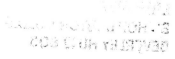

recording them and to be sensitive in assessing them. A relationship of trust and mutual respect, which has been much emphasised in this guide as characteristic of good practice, will be essential.

The curriculum is also distinctive in the following respects:

nature: by specifying learning outcomes it aims to avoid the criticism of woolliness often associated with personal development as an educational goal.

purpose: the key aim is to help all young people reach the thresholds of learning-readiness and/or job-readiness, so that they feel confident to take up opportunities now available to them.

focus: although it incorporates vital basic and key skills, the curriculum concentrates as much on feelings and attitudes – the domain of emotional literacy – as on knowledge and understanding

mode: it allows young adults to place learning outcomes in their context, by progressing through projects and learning activities in which they choose to take part.

control: both the selection of outcomes and the means of achieving them are determined by the young person, together with their mentor

assessment: the diverse forms of assessment can include self- and peer-assessment, as well as the use of a portfolio to record progress towards the agreed outcomes and a link with the new National Record of Achievement

context: it can be applied in a range of contexts which include informal settings as well as schools and colleges – youth projects, community service programmes, foyers, and so on.

Themes, learning outcomes and performance criteria

The curriculum comprises nine units based on themes identified in clusters in the three concentric circles set out below.

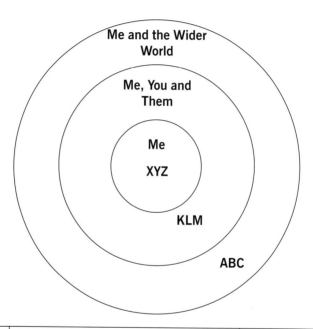

Units

A	Managing Yourself	Me and the
B	Using Information	Wider World
C	Exercising Rights & Responsibilities	
K	Handling Relationships	Me, You
L	Finding Support	and Them
M	Exploring Risks	
X	Knowing Yourself	Me
Y	Coping with Feelings	
Z	Holding Beliefs	

The innermost circle focuses on the inner world of the individual. Its main purpose is to enable the young person to tell their story in their words, to try and explain how and why they are the person they are. This is a challenging task but one that young people are likely to warm to, given the right encouragement. So many report that they have few opportunities to be listened to and recognised as unique individuals. This is their chance. There are two further units, one focusing on feelings and the other on beliefs. This gives young people the opportunity to explore their values and attitudes, how they have been formed and how they can change and develop. It encourages them to reflect and articulate and see the connections between feeling, thinking and action.

The intermediate circle focuses on relationships: with peers, adults and authority figures. It encourages young people to find out where they can go for support, how to ask the questions to which they need answers, to be clear and assertive in expressing their needs and how to get what they want from people without being aggressive or manipulative. It helps them understand the importance of respect for others and respect for themselves. And it provides a safe context in which to learn about the nature of risk-taking, and the possibilities and dangers which it offers.

The outer circle is closest to what are sometimes referred to as life and social skills. It gives young people the chance to explore and assess some of the situations they face in everyday life so that they can be more in control of events rather than their victim. It enables them to investigate the different varieties of information available to them to inform their decision-making and gives them the confidence to use them. And it introduces them to the range of responsibilities which attend the rights which come with adulthood. These three units abut and can be interwoven with the key skills contained within the national framework of qualifications.

It is important to emphasise that this curriculum is a framework not a syllabus. Like that under discussion with regard to Citizenship it specifies outcomes and criteria for assessment but does not tell teachers and informal educators what to do in order to achieve them. The defining feature of this curriculum is that the projects and activities through which the learning outcomes might be pursued should be determined in negotiation between the young person and the mentor. This seems to be a suitable way of learning some of the key attributes for living in a mature liberal democracy in the twenty-first century.

It will be for the young person and mentor together to determine an appropriate entry-point from among these units. They may decide it is prudent to start on the inner world and work outwards or vice-versa; or they may decide that the best place to start is on the relationships at home where the young person wants to see some change. It is essential that the young person and mentor are given complete discretion in determining how to proceed.

Set out overleaf is an illustration of how one of these themes can be ascribed learning outcomes and performance criteria by which they are assessed. Again, the learning outcomes are best achieved and assessed when they are contextualised within a project or activity.

Units: Using Information

Learning Outcomes	Performance Criteria
1. know where to go for information	1.1 formulate the questions to get the required information 1.2 record the answers given 1.3 plan how you will use the information 1.4 record what happens when you use the information
2. use a range of information to make a choice	2.1 make a preferred choice using the available information 2.2 record the consequences of your choice and how you felt about them 2.3 review the extent to which the information retrieved helped you make that choice 2.4 consider whether and how you might act differently in similar situations
3. use different forms of communication to convey information	3.1 communicate information in the manner chosen 3.2 record the consequences of doing this and how you felt about them 3.3 consider what you might do differently next time
4. present information about yourself to best advantage	4.1 plan and prepare a spoken and written presentation about yourself to a potential employer 4.2 make a spoken and written presentation about yourself to a potential employer 4.3 receive and discuss feedback 4.4 consider what you might do differently next time
5. recognise that gaining and using information can give you greater control over your life	5.1 plan how to collect useful information in order to solve a problem or achieve a goal 5.2 carry out the plan 5.3 record the outcomes and consider how successful the plan was

Conclusion

In this publication we have tried to draw attention not just to many exciting examples of effective and successful projects but also to a changing policy climate and some new curriculum thinking. There is a widespread and a high-level interest in the problems of youth disaffection and in the contribution which education initiatives might be able to make in addressing them.

We have outlined some of the key features of effective practice, principally the attributes, methods and approaches used by teachers and other practitioners in motivating young adults to learn and achieve. We have stressed the need for:

- a range of imaginative and innovative approaches to targeting and recruitment, including the use of outreach workers to make contact and incentives to draw young adults back into learning

- establishing activities which are intrinsically attractive and using these as hooks to secure the young adults' continuing involvement and their learning of key, vocational and practical skills

- negotiation, flexibility and differentiation in the development and provision of programmes

- open communication with learners based on trust and mutual respect

- small group sizes

- variation in pace and activity

- good quality, up-to-date environments for learning

- balance between individual and group learning

- continuous assessment, guidance and personal support of learners at all stages of the programme

- curricula which recognise strengths and areas for development, build self-esteem and enable learners to make choices and connections

- assessment and accreditation schemes which recognise a wide range of skills, knowledge, attitudes and attributes and which are not unduly bureaucratic for learners and practitioners

- close co-operation and the creation of partnerships between agencies in running and supporting programmes in order to bring a more holistic approach to the learning and development of young adults.

We believe that all young people – not just those who are disaffected and disengaged – deserve a curriculum to which they can connect their life and their world, and one which they can genuinely regard as an entitlement rather than a burden. It needs therefore to embody connectedness: between youth and adult roles; between learning and life; between feelings and thoughts; between words and actions; between processes and outcomes. We have outlined such a curriculum and showed its links to the current agenda of lifelong learning and active citizenship. Our main concern in this guide, however, has been that group of young people who feel excluded from the social mainstream. To meet their learning needs the concept of connectedness should have even more resonance.

At present educational underachievement and multiple disadvantages are not just closely linked but often handed down from one generation to the next. The circumstances in which people live obviously affect the life-choices they make, but in a democratic and technologically advanced society it is important that all citizens are able to make choices – to take the decisions which affect their lives and to take responsibility for the consequences. As educators we are usually unable to affect the social or family circumstances in which learners are living and growing; but we could certainly do more to offer a curriculum which permits young people to make choices, to build self-confidence and to see the connections between learning and a better life.

In this guide we have identified some quality educational programmes up and down the country which have proved attractive and stimulating for young adults on the margins of society and which have enabled many of them to make a new life. There are many more young people who need to be shown a way out of the cul-de-sac of low expectations and under-achievement and offered a route along the highway on which the rest of society is travelling.

Selected bibliography

Andersen Consulting, *The Attributes of Youth: Young people, education and employability*, 1998

Department for Education and Employment, *Equipping Young People for Working Life*, Consultative Document, 1996

Department for Education and Employment, *Maximising Potential: New Options for Learning After 16*, Consultative Document, 1996

Department for Education and Employment, *On Track – Motivating Young People to Stay in Learning*, Consultative Document, 1997

Department for Education and Employment, *Survey of Careers Service Work with Disaffected Young People*, Consultative Document, 1997

ECOTEC, *Evaluation of Initiatives Attracting Young People into Youth Training*, DfEE, 1997

Employment Policy Institute and Prince's Trust, *What Works? Jobs for Young People*, 1997

Employment Policy Institute and Prince's Trust, *What Works? The New Deal for Young People*, 1997

Hand J and Wright W, *Youth work in colleges: building on partnership*, FEDA, 1997

House of Commons Education and Employment Committee, *Disaffected Children*, 1998

Industry in Education, *Towards Employability*, 1996

Institute for Public Policy Research, *Wasted Youth: Raising Achievement and Tackling Social Exclusion Amongst 14-19 Year Olds*, 1998

Kennedy H, *Learning Works: Widening Participation in Further Education*, FEFC, 1997

Mid Glamorgan TEC, *16 and 17 Year Olds Not in Education, Training or Employment*, 1995

Northern Ireland Economic Research Centre and University of Ulster, *'Status 0': A Socio-Economic Study of Young People on the Margin*, Training & Employment Agency, 1997

Rathbone CI, Learning and Earning: Education, *Training and Employment for All in the 21st Century*, 1997

Reisenberger A and Crowther R, F*urther Education: Giving Young People a New Start*, FEDA/DfEE, 1997

South Glamorgan TEC, *Young People Not in Education, Training or Employment in South Glamorgan*, 1994

Training and Employment Agency (Northern Ireland), *Status 0: A Socio-Economic Study of Young People on the Margin*, 1997

TEC National Council Chief Executive's Network, *Disaffection and Non-Participation in Education, Training and Employment by Individuals Aged 18-20*, DfEE, 1996

West A and Ciotti M, *The New Start Strategy: Engaging the Community*, DfEE and Community Development Foundation, 1998

Wilkinson P, The Drop Out Society, *Young People on the Margin*, Youth Work Press, 1995

Youth Aid, *Taking Their Chances: Education, Training and Employment Opportunities for Young People*, 1995

Youth Work Press, The Carnegie Young People Initiative, Y*oung People as Citizens Now*, 1997

Youth Work Press, The Carnegie Young People Initiative, Y*ears of Decision*, 1997

Youth Work Press, The Carnegie Young People Initiative, *Good Work for Young People*, 1997

Contact names and addresses of case-studies

Stan Brocklehurst
Spilsby Youth Centre
Spilsby
Lincolnshire

Ian Carruthers
Youth Skills Preparation
Bolton College
Manchester Road
Bolton
BL2 1ER

Leigh Cook
Transitions into Work
4 Garlick Street
Oldham

Maureen Ireland
Development and Training Manager
YMCA
The Walk
Cardiff
CF2 3AG

Jill Kibble
Park Lane College
Cross Gates Centre
4th Floor, Arnedale House
Station Road
Cross Gates
Leeds
LS15 8EU

Pat Mannion
Hodge Hill and Yardley Youth Office
Ward End Park House
Ward End Park
Washwood Heath Road
Birmingham
B8 2HB

Mary McLoughlin
Training for Life
The Women and Girls Information
    Resource Centre
Peter Street
St Helens
Merseyside

Marilyn Morgan
Basic Skills Centre
Pontypridd College
Ynys Terrace Rhydyfelin
Pontypridd
CF37 5RN

Chris Peat
East Leeds Family Learning Centre
Brooklands View
Leeds
LS14 6SA

Debbie Roddam
Career Club
Interchange Centre
West Street
Gateshead
NE8 1BH

Louize Wagg
Daytime Potentials
Derby Youth House
Mill Street
Derby
DE1 1DY

Alison Wylde
Newham Docklands Motorcycle
    Project
NCFE
Woolwich Manor Way
London
E16 2QY